ABOUT THE AUTHOR

Clare likes to write poetry on various subjects including friendship, love and unrequited love, struggles with mental health issues, social issues, inclusivity and the power of individuality.

She grew up in Raheny and studied Irish and French at Trinity College Dublin.

Clare has had several poems published in magazines over the years, two short stories published in the *Womans Way* and also has written several memoir-type stories.

DEDICATION

Dedicated to my wonderful family.

I was a child once
I skipped and I played
Oh, how I yearn for those carefree days
The games in the garden
And the daisy chains that I made.

Clare O'Reilly

RAISED ON SONGS AND STORIES...

AUSTIN MACAULEY PUBLISHERS™
LONDON • CAMBRIDGE • NEW YORK • SHARJAH

Copyright © Clare O'Reilly (2021)

The right of Clare O'Reilly to be identified as author of this work has been asserted in accordance with section 77 and 78 of the Copyright, Designs and Patents Act 1988.

All rights reserved. No part of this publication may be reproduced, stored in a retrieval system, or transmitted in any form or by any means, electronic, mechanical, photocopying, recording, or otherwise, without the prior permission of the publishers.

Any person who commits any unauthorized act in relation to this publication may be liable to criminal prosecution and civil claims for damages.

A CIP catalogue record for this title is available from the British Library.

ISBN 9781398427112 (Paperback)
ISBN 9781398427129 (ePub e-book)

www.austinmacauley.com

First Published in this collection (2021)
Austin Macauley Publishers Ltd
25 Canada Square
Canary Wharf
London
E14 5LQ

ACKNOWLEDGEMENTS

I would like to thank my friends who have encouraged me and Dennis Grieg, of Lapwing Publications in Belfast who was also very supportive when I published some poems under my pen name 'Dawn Rock'.

PREAMBLE

It was inevitable that I would write poetry. My inspiration came from everything, from the nursery rhymes in early primary school to the hymns we sang at mass to the rock and pop songs of my teenage years. I was always writing lists of words that rhymed, the lyricism in them appealed to me. I remember that day in English class at 15 when I heard those words of Shakespeare:

'Not marble, nor the gilded monuments
Of princes, shall outlive this powerful rhyme;
But you shall shine more bright in these contents
Than unswept stone, besmear'd with sluttish time"

Sonnet 55

I really hoped that someday I would write a powerful rhyme, any rhyme. I was drawn to poetry.

Writing poetry is something I do when the humour comes on me, when inspiration strikes. If I feel strongly about something I write a poem about it. If I observe something or suffer something or something amuses me it can end up positively in a poem. I find it not only cathartic but empowering to be able to express myself in this way. To write it and to see the poem complete is rewarding in itself but to see it published is the ultimate achievement.

In College we had learned about the file/poet of old Ireland: he had a powerful role making his patron more popular with a good poem or drawing unfavourable attention upon him with a satire! The power a poet could have amused me no end. Oh, to be a poet indeed!

'Poeta nasictur,non fit' is the latin term for 'poets are born and not made' . I often wondered if I had been born this way or had simply picked up some tricks along the way.

Sometimes I feel that I express myself best through verse.

My themes include love and unrequited love, hopes, wishes and dreams, longings and disappointments with a number of dittys about shopping, diet and nights out!

I hope you enjoy this selection of my favourite poems. I also hope that you can identify with the girl of these verses and feel a connection with the themes expressed. Perhaps one of them will strike you as a 'powerful rhyme!'

POEMS

Who Would Have Thought…? 13

High and Low and No One Will Know 15

What's a Girl to Do? 16

A Friday Night 18

Castle 19

Antics 20

Milady 21

Full Story 22

A Mindfulness Reflection 23

A Prayer 24

Garden-Power 25

The Ballad of the Bold Brat and the Cailín Dána 26

This Girl 28

I Only Borrow 29

No More to Go 'on the Tear'! 30

What Does He Want? 32

O.M.G 33

Ode to John 34

Mad about me? 35

Tears on My Birthday 36

The Girl Who Cries on the Dart 37

No More to the Shops 38

To Help Me Improve My Diet 39

Some Office Girl! 40

Ducking and Diving 41

Such Witches 42

Such a Brat! 43

This Precious Jewel... 44

A Guy Who Really Cares... 45

A Bit on the Side 46

To Live just as I Dare! 47

Someone 48

Suddenly It's Over 49

An Tuath -v- an Cathair 50

Saol ait 51

Strange Life 52

Christmas Joy... 53

Ah, those Holidays in the Sun! 54

Worth their Weight in Gold 55

Not Define, but Confine! 56

These Two 57

At the Office 58

Smoking/Choking 59

Wish It Was Payday Every Day 60

A Tribute 61

Is Féidir Linn 62

Sunday Mornings 63

Who Would Have Thought...?

I would not have harmed myself
I would not have had the nerve to do something drastic
Like put a rope around my neck or a rolled-up sheet
Or swallow a bottle of pills
But in those bleak times
I would go to bed at night
And hope that I would not wake the next morning
And on waking my first thought would be
Oh No!
Not another day!
How will I bear it?
I call this passive suicide
The longing to just end
To give up the struggle and just sleep
To pass away without any effort
And when I was told I would have to get help
I resented it so – Why me? Why me?

Why me? – The seven year old girl with diabetes could say
Why me? – The teenager with epilepsy who cannot play football
 could say
I could not bear life in those days
I could not understand what all the excitement was about
I thought everyone was mad
I would perk up slightly as the day drew to a close
Sleep offered some measure of oblivion
And there was always the hope...

And then there was the tortuous dilemma
I wanted people to know how I suffered
But yet I could not bear their sympathy
I wanted people to know how much of an effort
Even the simplest things were for me
But I knew they would not understand
And there was a risk I would be shunned

Bad and all as things were, it would be
Somehow worse if certain people knew

I was in a sad and sorry state
It was heart-breaking for those who loved me
And I could still cry when I think of
That twenty-something suffering girl
To her the outlook seemed so bleak
She could see no happy times ahead
She just wanted to stay in her bed

This heavy cloud of woe and despair
Stayed around for many a year
But happily, oh joyfully it passed
And now we find her happier
Than anyone would have believed possible

The joy of wonderful nephews
The love they have brought into her life
The interest in singing and Gaeilge and beagnach gach rud*
The happy holidays with great friends
And the saol-celebrating† that never ends
The love that fulfils at long last
And the escape from a very trying past

So anyone who identifies with the girl of the early verses
I plead with you to hold on tight
Sit it out or sleep it out
But don't give up
I cannot say what life has in store for you
But all I say is: Thank God I didn't pass away.

---

*   *almost everything*
†   *life-celebrating*

High and Low and No One Will Know

I may go high and I may go low
But most people will never know
I still manage to put on a good show
I will smile politely and seem quite calm
No one will guess how tormented I really am

When I am low – I feel so hopeless
It's all despair – What a mess
And when I am high I feel so angry
I am tormented with way too much energy

Doctors may come and doctors may go
And what does it matter for all that they know?
Here I will be demented, persecuted and knowing no peace
No matter how much, the medication, they increase

So everyone has their problems and worries and cares
And God knows how they manage theirs
I will just have to struggle on as best I can
And hope that I can come up with some kind of superhuman plan

What's a Girl to Do?

I want to love him
I want to kiss him and only him
To close the door and hug him
And forget all the hurt, the pain
The ones who never rang again

I don't want to love him
I want to flirt and play
To enjoy an anonymous, exciting lay
Life is full of possibilities
Who will I meet when I go out?

I want to love him
I want to lie in his arms
And feel safe and warm
I want to get to know him, oh yes
And be known and understood by him

I don't want to love him
To risk my heart for just one
To grow to need and crave him
It's better to play around
And just not get tied down

Not many understand this
They think I'm just a fickle miss
A striapach,* slapper, flighty bitch
A fucked up, spoiled and pampered girl
Addicted to the social whirl

I cannot understand it either
It tears me in two – moithered!
It is so hard to meet the one
But hard as well to give up the fun
How I dread the humdrum…

* *hussy*

There's fun to be had in one night stands
In naughty texts and strangers' hands
In taking risks, cheating, two-timing
In encouraging admirers who can join the queue
Or hopping on brats who say they adore you

Is it childish? Is it shallow?
Why not love a decent fellow?
Love or Lust? Fun or Joy?
A person's heart is not a toy!

A Friday Night

They throng three-deep at the bar
I sigh 'cos I'm not served so far
At last, I make eye-contact with the barman
'When you're ready!' Now we'll get the drinks in!
I hesitate: can I even be heard?
Surely not, not a word!

There is no way through this crowd
To stand still is not allowed
Elbows are jabbing, drinks are spilling
And the place just keeps filling
I hear my favourite songs and great music
And wonder if the DJ will play that hit

Some people are dancing, trancing or romancing
Others are swaying, playing or straying
All these creatures of the night
Are such an end-of-the-week sight

And so it's time to party
Each and everyone so flirty
As the music gets louder
The crowd get rowdier
I lose myself in the magic of it
Spellbound and taken over by it!

Castle

Lovers may come and lovers may go
But I am Queen of this Castle
Men are fun and can leave me all aglow
But I could do without the hassle

I've met guys that were too nice and
I've met guys who treated me right
And there's been fellas who'd make me cry
After they'd made me feel so high

One night stands, not holding hands
That is what, for me, life plans
How many times did I give my number
Only to be ignored by yet another bummer?

So join the queue, you just might do
But the last laugh will always be on you
Lovers may come and lovers may go
But happiness does not depend on some so-'n'-so!

Antics

Let me tell you about the antics of this pair
Well… they always spend their nights on the tear
Will they ever get off this merry-go-around?
When will their feet ever touch the ground?

It's a constant round of dressing up
Bars and guys, lipstick, perfume and make-up
Hoping to meet the man of their dreams
But kissing many 'frogs' in between

What about all the fun they have
Flirting and smiling and having a laugh?
These girls get loads of attention
But please, a girl just needs one guy to concentrate on!

Milady

Nothing could make milady smile
She fretted and fumed all the while
She could not be content with the one
And (what's more) she could not meet the one!

When all the lords were at the dance
Around them she would shimmy and prance
O how she would flirt and joke and play
Tryin' her best to have her wicked way

Milady was not sixteen… not twenty nor even thirty
It was quite unseemly for her to be so flirty!
The best she could do now was to read and read
Her fun and adventure to be found in a book. Indeed…

Full Story

Nobody knows the full story
So much going on that they can't see
Your parents see a child they have raised and has made them proud
Your friends see a girl who stands out from the crowd
The guys see a woman that they desire
Employers see someone that they can hire
Colleagues may befriend you or keep their distance
Neighbours may help or mind their own business
Other people are so preoccupied
The world at large can't see inside

Sometimes you wonder can you even see the whole picture?
Can you understand, can you see what fits here?
It's not a puzzle to be solved in a day or two
It's the enigma that's so special, it's You!

A Mindfulness Reflection

Life can be crazy, each of us caught up in the daily grind
But we must set aside some precious time to protect the mind
As we try to balance work, home and social demands
We find that we have a massive struggle on our hands

Do not be afraid, just stop and look around you
You are part of a great plan, reflected in all you do
Just pause and give yourself a chance to see
What is before you and how great life can be!

A Prayer

When it seems like this world makes no sense at all
And I wonder what we are all struggling for
There are people praying for me
Protecting me from things I cannot see

This is such a source of comfort
To know such love – a refuge from hurt
They allay my fears, chase away my tears
And are there for me throughout the years

Support and advice along the way
Is kindly dispensed every day
A blessing, given freely, given often
Let me reflect on that when things are so uncertain

Garden-Power

She looked out on the garden
A kaleidoscope of colours greeted her gaze
This was no orderly nor 'neat and tidy' garden
Her eye ran here and there
The flowers had been planted in a helter-skelter fashion
And mirrored the emotions that ran amok within her
But then the peace, oh the peace
To sit here quietly and gaze upon such beauty
It was purely exquisite!

The Ballad of the Bold Brat
and the Cailín Dána*

It must have started in about 2003...

There was the flirting in Tamangoes,
And he asked for her number (many times)
Tho' she tried not to encourage him,   2004
She could not help smiling at him,
It was only going to be a matter of time...

Then there was that night in Bojangles   2005
Oh the dancing and the attention
It just drove her wild
And what about the kiss in his car
On the way home that night?

She found him hard to resist
But what about all the guilt?
Nonetheless he continued to woo her
There were funny little texts
And visits to her Castle

And then one night he came to Sands Bar   2006
To hear her sing
And it wasn't long after that
'til this affair became the real thing!

She struggled with her guilt and from time to time
She would say we must stop
And he would joke and say, 'Am I getting sacked again?'
She also struggled with her highs and lows
But he had a way of dealing with that.

This affair is hot...
They really should not   2007

*   *bold / daring girl*

The texts that they send are X-rated
And the sex leaves them both elated
But what can become of this sort of thing?
It can only ever be a fling!

Sequel

But by 2008...
The Cáilín Dána was in a right ol' state
This was not a guy that she could ever date
He would never be a proper mate
If this continued, the Bold Brat she would only hate
So she thought: *Get out now before it's too late!*

However, this was not the end of this pair
About each other they continued to care
Throughout 2009 a friendship so deep
They both so carefully managed to keep
Thoughts, ideas, fears and dreams they continued to share   *2010*

And so far as we know they are still in touch
And really care about each other very much   *to date...*

This Girl

Oh there was this lovely girl
But why did she run herself down?
And why did she so often frown?
Her blessings were many
And her friends were plenty
Yet she longed for a man who would date her
And the happiness that this would create for her

If only she could appreciate
Life as it was without a mate
Her lovely house and lifestyle
But no, she was in denial
Instead of enjoying her freedom
She constantly yearned to meet him

The man of her dreams was all she could think of
And sometimes she would even break down and sob
What is to become of me all alone and getting older?
She just could not accept that there was no man for her

In the meantime there were those all around who envied her
Thought how lucky she was to have no man near her
The house to herself, she could do as she please
Come and go, suit herself, live a life of ease

Content with her lot, this girl was not
A problem for mankind since the year dot
But perhaps she could learn from the lessons of the past
And rather than pine for what she has not – enjoy what she has!

I Only Borrow

I never steal
I only borrow
How could that cause any sorrow

He comes to see me
But does he really get me
All so quick, he leaves me

I have some fun
But when we're done
I never end up feeling like: I'm 'the one'

I never steal
I only borrow
How could that cause so much sorrow

No More to Go 'on the Tear'!

Sadly she started to drink too young
And so into chaos and turmoil was flung
No matter what problems it brought about
The alcohol she could not go without!

It made her gregarious which she thought hilarious
And let her be outrageous and so courageous
If something was funny she laughed too loud
But if it was sad she cried out loud
And it was not unusual for her to get angry
The exaggeration of emotion was really quite scary!

While the hangovers she suffered were such a curse
Other side effects were so much worse
On the night she'd be flyin'
The next day she'd be cryin'
And for days on end she'd be generally dyin'

Tho' this pattern emerged and the link was clear
She continued to drink for many a year...

All in all the booze caused her nothing but trouble
It could freak her out 'n' even worse burst her bubble
When under the influence she'd be all in a muddle
And you'd never know who she might 'cuddle'

There was that time when she was so jarred
That she caused a furore and got herself barred...

Whether she got randy on brandy or frisky on whisky
The whole business was really quite risky
On the wine she felt she would have a good time
Oh the self-deception... it was such a crime

If they thought she was a slapper
For going out on the batter
What did she care? – She could almost roar
Much more fun to be considered a goer than a bore!

How great it must be when you can enjoy a drink
To relax with two or party with a few...
But if your health is to suffer...
... then why would you bother?

What Does He Want?

All he wants is a sex goddess
All dolled up in a glamorous dress
But little attention he will pay
Until the night is well under way

When the pints are in
That's when he will begin
To strut about and start to flirt
With many girls for all he's worth

But on and on he'll knock the pints back
Thinking that they are all having the crack
But that's not the case unfortunately
And the night is sure to end in misery

For the girls realise in good time
That this guy is just p*ssed out of his mind
And so he is left all alone
Searching about for his mobile phone!

O.M.G.

O.M.G. the attention guys will pay
When tryin' to have their wicked way
The compliments, the treats, the lies
They'll even look deep into your eyes!

But watch out girl, play it cool
You don't want to be just anyone's fool
If he goes the distance, means what he says
You will soon suss him out and figure his ways

Enjoy the crack and have good fun
But don't think too soon that you're the 'one'
For that is the road to misery
And you'll end up truly weary
If you take my advice and keep the head
He will end up cracked about you instead!

Ode to John

I often think of him
Too often…
Considering I haven't seen him in over fifteen years
Is he married now?
Still living in London?
Does he still wear his hair long?
Did he ever write that book?
Did I feature in any way?
Does he ever think of me?
Will I ever bump into him again?
Would it be good for me?
He wrecked my head – so he did!
We fought more than anything
Oh – it was so passionate….
I suppose he hurt me most
By inviting my sister to a Chris de Burgh concert
But I got him back by snogging his best friend.

And then he 'diagnosed' me as suffering
From the 'hula' bird syndrome
Who apparently flies around and around
Until it flies up its own ass!!
Maybe he had a point
For these and many other reasons
He stands out in my memory!

Mad about me?

He was mad about me
He told me so regularly
And then one day I heard him say
About a group of us
'Let's face it,' he said
'There's none of us oil paintings'
That couldn't include me, I thought
But it did
I just didn't feel the same about him
Or anything after that
He was mad about me
And even he didn't think I was pretty
On the bad days that really didn't help
And on the good days
It brought me up short.

Tears on My Birthday

I got many lovely texts
and cards and good wishes
and calls and pressies
everyone really made such a fuss of me
You'd think I'd be happy
But no, there were tears on my birthday!

Was it because I was older
That guy didn't love me
I'd never have a baby
Or no one could save me
It's hard to understand
But when I should have been happy
There were tears on my birthday!

The Girl Who Cries on the Dart

There is this girl that I see on the train
She is quite pretty but it is such a shame
That she looks so sad and she often cries
What causes the sadness behind those eyes?

I've seen her smile and even laugh
When a friend and herself are having a chat
But far too often she can't keep the tears in
When she's alone and quiet and must be thinkin'

She hides it well – does not make a scene
Most would not even notice …
But I have spotted how she surreptitiously wipes the tears away
Then gathers up her things and goes about the rest of her day

No More to the Shops

a.k.a. how to survive the recession...

Enough of the silly dresses
And the shoes that I can't walk in
Enough of all this dashing about town
And the prices that just make me frown

Let me now enjoy what I have in my collection
Take my time with each interesting and exciting selection
Celebrate each colour
Regard each style
And congratulate myself on such good taste

Team up those 4-year-old jeans with last year's top
Jazz up that coat with that hat you thought was such a flop!
Search to the back of your wardrobe for the treasures you are sure to find there
Get them all out and give them another fab 'n' fun wear!

Okay so things are tight
But we are going to be alright
We can be resourceful
And still have our wardrobes full!

To Help Me Improve My Diet...

No more to indulge my sweet-tooth!
Sugar is my downfall, to tell the truth.
It goes straight to my waist
So as much as I love the taste
That's an end to the cakes and treats for me!

As the pounds pile on
I cannot simply munch on
And when the spots begin to appear
More chocolate will not make them disappear
I will have to mend my ways, I fear!

The cravings I will have to manage
Instead of acting like a savage
Self-control can be exercised
And thus health and beauty realised

Fit and slim I will be
Clear of skin with so much energy
'What is her secret?' all will wonder
As joy and an inner glow radiate from her!

Some Office Girl!

I'm not cut out for life at the Office
I see myself as a far more glam miss
Maybe a singer, oh I'd be on to a winner
Or maybe one who writes and can set some sights
Maybe a dancer, Oh what a chancer!

But not this penance of 9 to 5
Where I am either scared or bored alive
I'm no good with files – what goes in never comes out again
And as for computers – I'm just terrified of them
When the boss begins to speak, I begin to panic
If I have to remember all that, I'll surely go manic
So when I'm supposed to be typing
I'm really romancing – I'm on *Strictly Come Dancing*
Instead of working things out on the calculator
I imagine I'm going to be a wow on *X- Factor*

So when it comes to 5 o clock
I'm in for a shock
My in-tray is full of demands
All work is still on-hands
My dreams may have entertained me
But I have to stay late to clear the necessary!

Ducking and Diving

You'll have to put a stop to all this ducking and diving
It'll finish you off: all this treacherous conniving
No more of your stories, no more of your lies
Your future in truth and integrity lies...

And no longer to be such a two faced b*tch
Smiling like you agree but secretly making a switch
Be straight, come clean for no good can come of your double-dealing
The new approach you take will lead to your longed-for healing!

Such Witches

Dear girl, why surround yourself with such b*tches?
They should all be burned at the stake like witches
Hangin' around with them has become such a pain
Your face is beginning to show the strain

When you are in trouble – do they give a damn?
Their concern and pity – it's all a sham
Don't be deceived, they're enjoyin' the show
Waiting and watching for your tears to flow

It's time to get wise
Give them all a big surprise
Find your cop-on
And yes, move on!

Such a Brat!

How I remember the night we first met
He so adorable, such a brat
Yes so full of charm
Out to tease and to disarm

We had a little dance
Oh, he had his chance
But 'No not a date,' he said
'Come on back to my place instead'

Now they all try it on, that's true
But this guy could really tempt you
Hold out for the date, I thought;
We all know what he thought!

Eighteen months the stand-off lasted
We'd meet up often but only flirted
Then in Gibney's Garden, one night, he asked
And my number to him, in a tizzy, I passed

But the boldest brat rang as I reached my door
And it wasn't long 'til he was on his way over
We had a night of fun
And then he was gone

And so it continued on, no date – just a chat in the bar
We were friends but it was never going to go far
But as the friendship continues to deepen…
Who knows what may happen?

This Precious Jewel...

So many years she had dedicated to this guy
But now it was no use all she could do was cry
How quickly he could forget her
And move on like he had never met her

Alas that was the end to her hopes and dreams
Her life now seemed to be coming apart at the seams
Not a bother on him though, he just carried on
Like 'What's your problem? I've done nothing wrong'

But life has a way of working things out
And it's interesting yet strange how it changes about
For this guy will surely rue the day
That he let this precious jewel slip away!

A Guy Who Really Cares...

So there was this guy out Malahide way
I used to meet up with on a Friday
Flirting and teasing and all the banter
Lots of fun and lots of laughter

Oh yes, he had his chance
But me he did not romance
So now he can chat away
But little attention I will pay!

Instead I plan to meet someone new
My partner in crime says, 'It's about time too'
I won't entertain them unless they knock me down
With compliments and treats and take me out on the town

They better pay attention to my every need
Show that they are interested and take heed.
There's no point in lacklustre love affairs:
Please Lord, send me a guy who really cares!

A Bit on the Side

A bit on the side, I shall be no more
I'll just point my Manolo Blahniks towards the door
When they start with that talk
I'll just take a walk
I'm serious, I tell you
I'll just start anew

If they can't take me out on a date
I won't even wait
To hear that it's complicated, this or that,
I'll just turn them down flat

Here comes a New Year
And I shall be of good cheer
With this bright new attitude
I'll attract myself a mighty fine dude!

To Live just as I Dare!

You expect me to report my every move
What will that tell, what will it prove?
My comings and goings, I have to justify
As to my spending, you I have to pacify

Can't you see that this is so unfair
I need to live just as I dare
The longer I remain under your control
The more I damage my very soul

I cannot be your 'puppet-on-a-string'
I was born to 'do-my-own-thing'
Let me have some room to breathe
I have my own life to lead...

Someone

You'd think that you would know someone
When you have shared the fun
The laughter and the tears
All throughout the years

But people have different dreams and drives
Fears and secrets that shape their lives
Don't imagine you have someone figured out
And actually know what they are about.

They may seem to confide in you
And indeed all they say is true
But you are not privy to what is going on
And cannot even guess at what might be wrong

Suddenly It's Over

And so it's cosy chats, lingering looks and tender kisses
Holding hands, whispered promises and realised wishes
You tell each other every little thing
Maybe even wear one another's ring

Not a moment goes by but you share something new
He wonders how he ever lived without you!
The fun, the laughter, the revelry,
The weekends, the holidays, the company…

Then suddenly it's over
Not a word!

An Tuath -v- an Cathair

An Ceathrú Rua:
Aer brea folláin
Boladh an fhairraige
Na héin ag canadh
Na beacha ag crónán
Mise i m'aonar ar an mbóthar
      go sona sásta!

Báile Átha Cliath:
Trácht
Truailliú
Torann!

TRANSLATION: *The Country -v- the City*

Carraroe:
Grand fresh air
The smell of the sea
The birds singing
The bees humming
And I all alone on the road, quite happy!

Dublin:
Traffic
Pollution
Noise!

Saol ait

Ar an Luan tagann sí ar ais ón tuath,
Ar an Máirt téann sí go sochraid
Ar an gCéadaoin bíonn slaghdán uirthi
Ar an Déardaoin tagann sí isteach (ag a ceathair!!!)
Ar an Aoine bíonn sí ag feitheamh ar fhear a' phoist

Is nach amhlaidh den seachtain mar a shíneann sí go bliain

Lá amháin tá an ola imithe, lá eile níl an teas ag obair
Anois is arís bíonn sí ag fanacht ar ghlaoch
Go rialta bíonn rud eile i gceist,
Ach is annamh a thagann sí isteach

Bíonn sí ina codladh ag meán lae agus ar an nguthán ag meán oíche
Nuair a chuireann sí glao, bíonn an fón i gcónaí gafa
Nuair a chuireann sí litir sa phost, téann sí ar strae
Gach uair a chuireann sí glaoch ort, bhí sí ag iarraidh teacht ort níos
  túisce
Agus gach uair a thugann tú teachtaireacht di, bhí sí ag plé leis cheana

Ach cad a dhéanann sí nuair a bhíonn an doras dúnta
Agus cad é an boladh láidir sin?
Cad tá faoi cheilt aici sna cófraí?
An bhfuil a fhios ag éinne nó an bhfuil siad go léir ag cur i gcéill go
  bhfuil gach rud ceart go leor
Tá gach rud ceart go leor? Ní cheapaim é!

TRANSLATION

A poem about working with an alcoholic, the excuses they come up, the poor attendance and sometimes others bury their heads in the sand while the drinker continues to hide and hide...

Strange Life

On a Monday, she has better things to do
On a Tuesday, she goes to a funeral
On a Wednesday, she has a cold
On a Thursday, she comes in, (but at 4pm!)
On a Friday, she must wait at home for the postman

And that continues, until the weeks become months, then a year!

One day the oil is gone, another the heating is not working
Sometimes she has to wait at home for a call
Often, there is something up
But rarely does she come in!

She sleeps 'til midday and tries to contact colleagues at midnight
When she makes a call, the phone is mostly engaged
When she posts a letter, it goes astray
When she rings you, she was usually trying to get you earlier
And when you give her a message: 'Oh I've dealt with that already!'

But what does she do when the door is closed
And what is that strong smell?
What is hidden in the presses
Does anyone know or are they all pretending that everything is OK?
Everything is OK? I don't think so!

Christmas Joy...

It was coming up to Christmas, the cards were piling in
Trees were going up all around with lights a twinklin'
Children were getting so excited, even adults too
Everyone was all agog, about their Christmas do!

Santa's letter had been written in every house in town
Favourite Christmas songs playin', to make a smile of each frown
'Have a good one' people wished each other with good cheer
And hoped all good things ahead for the New Year

But many were struggling to put on a brave face
And get through the season with as much good grace
The separated father who would not see his little one
Or the guy who sleeps on our streets at night, he has no home!

Or the guy who had buried his dad last month
Or the girl who had lost her baby – due this month
Or one of the many who has a very sad story to tell
But does not, and instead, at Christmas time, smiles and wishes you well!

So think of these people as you put on the lights
And send them a wish or a prayer
And hope that somehow, this year, in your
Joy and happiness, they will share!

Ah, those Holidays in the Sun!

For some the holidays start when they begin to pack
It's all excitement with no thoughts of coming back!
Others unwind when they get to the airport
And there are those who love to start on the plane
While some love to get to the beach or the sea
Wherever it starts it has to be fun and carefree!

The ladies like nothing better than to shop
And on holidays they never seem to stop
So many gems, shoes, bags and other goodies on offer
Something for sure for the bargain hunter!

For sure, we love the gorgeous meals and lovely food
On holidays, relaxed, we've never felt so good
The tasty breakfasts and afternoon teas
The restaurants where we are treated like VIPs

So whether it's lying in the sun
Or going for breakfast before one
Dancing the night away
Or taking a trip around the bay

While there is camping and skiing trips, safaris and treks, cruises and you name it
It's a holiday in the sun for us or forget it!

Worth their Weight in Gold...

We all know one
We wonder why they do it
It can't be for the money
It's certainly not for the glory
But we all depend on them

They are first to hold you when you're a baby
They mind you when you're old
And at every stage in between, they are there for you
Nurses are worth their weight in gold

So, this dispute must be resolved
All of society is involved
I urge the Government through these verses
Just think, how your friends and families need the nurses!

Not Define, but Confine!

And so, we have my creative side
My fun-loving side
The part of me that just loves to get up and go out for a walk!
The gallivanter
The girl who likes to dance all night
And flirt with the guys
To chase a butterfly with her eyes
Or admire a night sky full of stars
To roam the fields and admire the wild flowers
To go out without a coat and dodge the showers!
To write a poem that will delight and please her
And meet a friend who will understand and inspire her
So while this job of mine does not define me
It does at times rather confine me!

These Two...

There was a lot of hesitation
This guy was filled with reservation
She was lovely but a little unusual too
He really did not know what to do!

The attraction was very strong between them
Yet the least thing could really throw them
They longed to be together when they were apart
But when they were together things just drove them apart!

It was off and on all the year long
Where on earth were they going wrong?
But with her and her nerves, and him quite fond of the drop...
They needed to find a way and let the nonsense stop

If they were to be together, and be true to themselves and each other...
Things would have to settle down, there could not be so much bother,
They had such laughs, such fun, and the sex was off the Richter scale!
There was no way that these two should let this love between them fail!

At the Office

At the Office, each day, she tries and tries
But it is no use – she is always up to her eyes!
She tidies her desk as often as she can
And makes lists in her diary, well that's the plan

But in no time at all, the desk is up in a heap
And in queries and problems, she is knee-deep
How to sort it all out, she really wonders
She could do without all these mistakes and blunders!

It's getting her down, draining her energy
Something's gotta be done, we must find a remedy
She'd like to win the lotto, sure we all would
Strike it lucky somehow, escape if we could

But on and on she must go with the daily grind
And enthusiasm, strength and sense of humour find
She has many a year to go before she can get out
So enough of her complaining, she may leave it out!!

Smoking/Choking

When you think about this business of smoking
People choking
They have got to be joking!
If that is how they cope
They (and the rest of us) really have no hope
It's not only Mr I. Smoke who is affected!
Just think of how the whole room, space or car is polluted!

It is time to get serious about the ban
Some smoking areas are such a sham
If it is killing one in two
Someday soon that could be
Me or You!!!

Wish It Was Payday Every Day

On payday, she's a happy girl
Around the shops in such a whirl
A lovely lunch, coffee with a friend
Her money on treats, she loves to spend

Remember that top in M & S
Or what about that lovely dress?
There's make-up, lipstick, shoes and bags
To team up with her own glad rags

But then the bills, oh what a fright!
For she is going out on the town tonight
So soon she finds the money runs out
And she has plenty to fret and worry about

No money left for what she needs
Now she can rue her costly deeds
But it's no good, the money's all spent
On treats galore is where it went

So now she will have to exist on a fiver
Make it last for days, be a real survivor
Why does she let this happen time after time?
Putting herself thru' this – it is such a crime!

A Tribute

It's Páirc an Chrócaigh on Saturday, September 28th, 2013
We stand and show our respect for Amhráin na bhFiann*
The President then shakes the hand
Of each player from two of the finest hurling teams in the land

The crowd are cheering, smiling, waving, holding banners high
No opportunity to support their own side is let slip by
'Come on the Banner!' all the Clare people shout
While a roar from the rebel county rings loudly out

We are here to see the Liam Mc Carthy Cup come to Clare
We truly believe that it rightfully belongs there
Davy Fitzgerald and his team gave Cork hell the last day
Today the Clare lads are determined to go all the way

Three goals scored by Clare in the first twenty minutes
What a cracking pace and their hearts really in it
With Clare four points ahead by half time
To be robbed of this now would be a crime

But Cork picked up and then they were level
And for a while it seemed like the game was not going well
Then the pace picked up, the game could go either way
More goals for each side, points too, but Clare led the way
Clare widened the gap, kept the pressure on
And were victorious, what a game they won

Tús maith† made for a spectacular finish
There'll be celebrations galore this week in Ennis
They played their hearts out, to themselves were true
And that is why we can proudly say: An Clár Abú!‡

Published in the Clare Champion *at the time, September 2013*

* the National Anthem
† a good start
‡ Up Clare!

Is Féidir Linn

There is dread, there is fear,
All hoping the virus won't come near,
We're washing our hands until they're sore
Kissing, hugging and hand-shaking no more!

As they try to contain the virus,
All sorts of fears surround us
Conspiracy theories abound
Craziness, all around

If the coronavirus doesn't get you, the hysteria will
We hope and pray for a vaccine soon for this ill
But remember we are resilient
And a cure could be heaven-sent

We can get through this,
Is féidir linn!
To feel sorry for ourselves would be a sin
So draw on your strength deep within
Stay hopeful and try to enjoy staying in!

Sunday Mornings

When I was a child
I loved Sunday mornings
They were full of excitement
Mass was the place to be
Everyone went along
The sense of celebration was strong

I remember how we prayed
Children had to be well-behaved
The altar and the ceremony and the importance of being on time
Talking in the Church was frowned upon
All the standing and kneeling and the responses
Communion and Confirmation were a serious business
And the singing: the beautiful hymns
It was all so impressive…

But now Sundays sadden me
When I go to Mass, few are there
To see one of my peers is rare
The scandals have taken their toll
Vocations have dwindled to such a low

I would like to go to Mass more often
But I miss how it was back then
All of us sharing and yes…
It was good to meet everyone.